T0380870

Copyright © 2020 by Ann Coleman. 580292

All rights reserved. No part of this book may be reproduced
or transmitted in any form or by any means, electronic or
mechanical, including photocopying, recording, or by any
information storage and retrieval system, without permis-
sion in writing from the copyright owner.

This is a work of fiction. Names, characters, places and
incidents either are the product of the author's imagination
or are used fictitiously, and any resemblance to any actual
persons, living or dead, events, or locales is entirely coinci-
dental.

To order additional copies of this book, contact:
Xlibris
844-714-8691
www.Xlibris.com
Orders@Xlibris.com

ISBN: Softcover   978-1-4363-8961-7
       Hardcover   978-1-4363-8962-4
       EBook   978-1-6641-4634-1

Library of Congress Control Number: 2008911191

Print information available on the last page

Rev. date: 12/02/2020

I awoke on the morning of October 17, 1999 rather suddenly. _____ I work twelve hour shifts at a rehab facility while attending nursing school full time. This has been in progress for about seven years and I somehow see the light at the end. To purposely misquote Murphy's Law "Everything that can go wrong has – to prevent me from obtaining my nursing degree. Last evening, while at work, I picked up a copy of Juanita Bynum's book entitled "No Sheets". As I began to read the words, I found myself so engaged that I could not put it down. The words seemed to parallel my life and further inspired me to write my own book to encourage women of God to continue in their endeavors of preaching and teaching the Word of God.

Most stories begin with "once upon a time" but this is not a fairy tale, so I will begin with "My life as a woman preacher" this very phrase conjures up such symbolisms as rejection, shunning, criticism, disbelief and lack of confidence. My life as a woman preacher has been very devastating in many ways, but I will begin by guiding you through the process of getting to where I am today.

I as on my third marriage and my husband had to relocate as a result of his job. We moved from Donaldsonville to Thibodeaux. Donaldsonville is a little city or town between New Orleans and Baton Rouge, Louisiana. This is home for me. I was born here some forty-six years ago. I have lived in some other cities, but always made my way back here, my home. I had two daughters before this marriage and my son was born during this marriage. At this time he was about five or six months old. I was walking my girls to the bus just before the birth of my son and I met a white woman named Beverly. She began to talk to me about God. I loved talking about God, so we became very good friends. She lived in a little mobile home, only two rooms. I would go to her house and we discussed God and His Word. She gave me some teaching tapes to listen to. I cannot remember by whom, but I became very interested in the messages on the tapes. Beverly told me that she believed God had an important job for me to do. I told my husband that something different was happening to me. I felt connected to God, I had been saved since 1972, well, and I thought I was, but I never felt God's presence like this before and I loved the connection. So, I prayed most of the time, I read the Bible and listened to the teaching tapes. I could not explain what was happening to me, but I knew I found that God was not this big might person way up above us, but a loving Father, living within me.

I continued to get closer to God. After a while, still looking for a church to worship, I started working, at a hospital, twenty minutes from Thibodaux, in Houma, Louisiana. I met a Caucasian woman named Carline and we became instant friends. She invited me to church. I had attended Holiness Churches before so it was not a big deal to me. I felt that God was wherever and everywhere. I eventually became a member at this Pentecostal Church. It was and interesting experience. I became even closer to God. I prayed three times a day for long periods of time. I read my Bible and studied very hard. Even thought the white people in this church was under the impression that I was dumb and only white persons could teach me, they had nothing to do with my learning. It was as if the Hold Spirit just began to open my understanding to the Scripture. I would read and the Holy Spirit would interpret it for me. I would get visions of what it meant.

Strange things began to happen to me. When I would go to worship service or Bible study, and even prayer meetings, things would happen that I did not quite understand. I guess I need to give some examples to make this clearer. One night at worship service, I was on my knees praying quietly in tongues because I would not pray in tongues aloud unless there was an interpreter, even in the Pentecostal Church. If there was no interpreter, then God had nothing to say, I only would edify myself. However, I began to see visions. I would look at some people in the church and see then doing something else. One time I looked at one of the sisters and I saw her husband beating her and the children. About a month later she moved out of town and revealed to the church that her husband had been beating her and the children for years. She had kept this secret for many years. I had shared this vision with Carline. On another occasion a minister, I might add, he was considered very important to the church, he was preaching and I could see him laughing and cursing. A little while after the vision, one of my brothers came to fellowship with us, to his surprise this preacher worked with my brother. My brother said he was shocked to learn that brother was a preacher because he cursed so much on the job. There were many occasions, but when I saw the sister cheating on her husband, I said, "Lord why are you telling me these people's business?" Well, God only wanted me to know about his gifts and also that everything that looks like gold is not gold.

I continued to go to this church. I would commune with my brother Joseph about what was happening to me. On another occasion, the Holy Spirit told me that Joseph would pastor our home church. He totally rejected this because he hardly attended the church. I just told him what the Holy Spirit said to me. He has been pasturing at that church for thirteen years.

There was a time we went on a fast for some reason and we would pray every day at noon. I would go to my bedroom and kneel down at the foot of my bed and pray awhile. One day I went in to pray at noon, a very bright light came through the ceiling of my bedroom I jumped up and left the room and did not return to finish my prayers. I was very scared, but I did not tell anyone. The next day at noon, I went in to pray. Again just as I started to pray, the light started to shine through the ceiling. I thought well, I have to see this through. I cannot keep running. I did not run away. I just sat at the foot of my bed trembling with my hair raised on my head and arms. I felt frozen and not able to move or speak. Then the light became brighter and a voice filled the room. The voice said stand up. I stood up, my legs felt disjointed. I was scared, but the voice spoke so loudly like nothing I have ever heard. Then all of a sudden a Bible just appeared in mid air and the voice said "you see that bible?" I said yes. Then the voice said, "I want you to teach and preach my Word." At that moment, I knew it was God. I felt safe. Then the voice of God said, "I want you to preach and teach my Word. I will exalt you. I will make you great. I will put you places where no one can touch you, but teach and preach my word." Then another very strange thing happened during this time. My mother had been dead for many years by 1982. She appeared in the corner of my room by the closet. She never spoke a word. The voice spoke, "Do you see your mother over there?" just nodded my head, yes. He went on so say that she will live in you and at that point, she walked over to me and went inside of my body. Then I became weak because I knew she was dead. The voice repeated, "Go preach and teach my Word. I told my husband when he came home from work. He became frightened and told me that this is the reason that he cannot deal with that God stuff He did not live for the Lord.

I at this point, called Joseph, my brother, and told him what had happened. He did not say much about it except assured me that God had not called me to preach. I believed I had misunderstood because of what I had been taught. It was told to all women that only men was to preach, never women I had been told that woman was not important to God. As a matter of a fact, I can record being told that a woman was so sad. It was a curse to be a woman. I was told over and over how we (my brothers) should not have any sisters. They wish they did not have a sister at all. There was no respect for females from my brothers. When they spoke of the Coleman's, they referred to the males. Because they believed they are the only things important. I have no idea where this attitude surfaced from, but it is there in my brothers. It does not matter what a female does, she can accomplish anything she desires, and my brothers ignore it unless it is a male.

I have some nieces that have accomplished great things, but it is not heard of in my family because it was one of the girls so this is not important. Now out of this kind of environment, God calls me to preach. This went against the grain in my family.

Soon after my calling, my husband left me and I moved back to Donaldsonville. It was ignored what I had shared with the family about my calling, so I ignored it too. For some years, I just studied the Word and did some teaching.

I met Curtis sometimes after Lionel left me; and we were married. I continued to study and teach others the Word of God. Finally one day, just out of the blue, I got a headache. The pain was so bad, I became very confused and my husband told me I tried of jump out of the car on the way to the hospital.

When we arrived at the hospital, the pain was so great; I could hear a fly as if he had giant wings. At this time, I was in the emergency room; and the doctors thought I was a drug addict. One of the nurses came in not aware that I had studied nursing, gave me a short of normal saline. If the pain had gone away, then they would have been sure I was a drug user. However, while the doctors and nurses were playing their little game, the pain became so bad, I ran out of e emergency: room to the side of the hospital. I leaned against the building and began to pray. I said, "God what is wrong?" You always hear me or you make the pain bearable. What is it, Lord"? The Lord began to speak to me. He said, "I needed to get your attention. You have disobeyed me. I told you to preach and teach my word." I said, "Lord, I am a woman and women are not allowed to preach." God said, "I told you to preach and teach my word." He went on to say to me. "If you do not preach and teach my Word, I will take your life and bring you home with me." I responded, Lord, what should I do?" The Lord said, "Preach and teach my Word." The Lord caught me up in a vision and carried me back to the vision in my bedroom when I was called to preach and teach. God allowed me to see the same vision again; and then he reminded me that I said to teach and preach and I will open doors. I will exalt you. I will take you places where no one can touch you. Preach and Teach my word, said the

Lord. I said, "Yes Lord, I will teach and preach your Word." The pain in my head did not leave right away and now I know why. If the pain had gone away then, I would have been labeled as a drug addict.

When the doctor returned or the nurse asked me if my pain was better, I responded by saying, "If you would have given me some pain medicine, maybe it would be better. Saline will not stop this pain in my head." At this point, I was given some pain medicine. Then the pain became tolerable. After an hour of so, we started back home. I talked to my husband. He told me he would support me while I work in the ministry I was given. Then it began. Everything, everyone, every loved one began to see me in a different light. I found myself at odds with everyone without saying or doing anything. It appeared everywhere I went I was hated.

I must take a little time to talk about this one brother, I will call Sam, who I loved very much. We were always close as we grew up. For some reason we had much in common. We just kind of clicked with each other. I loved all of my brothers, but we had something special. He had a way that made me feel I can do anything. He would spend time with me. He would give me money and buy me clothes. We had a special closeness.

When we got saved it was the same time. He was called to preach. My older brother did not have confidence in him to be a preacher. I told him God called preachers, not men. I encouraged him to go on. I was always there for him and with him. There was a time when he and I were the only two in the family that went to church besides my daddy. Every time he would talk of giving up, I was there to push him. Whatever he did, I was there to push or pull him. Along the way, I wanted him to be very successful. Finally he became just that.

We would go to church to fellowship with other sisters and brothers and find them abusing the women ministers. Most of the preachers would treat them so very bad. Sam and I had the opportunity to see some ministers we regarded with high respect misuse female ministers. Sam told me on several occasions, "I would never treat a woman like that." I believed him, not knowing that I would become one of these ministers.

As time went on, my brother, Jim, decided to join in with us. He started to come to church with us. Before you knew it, Sam had started to treat me badly. It took me a while to realize he was mistreating me because I could not see any reason. So, I would just ignore it when he stood me up when I was supposed to go to church with Jim and him.

Sam and I had studied together for a long time before Jim joined in with us. Then, he did not want me to study with them anymore. He would ask me what nights I had something to do and he would put Bible Study or whatever was going on for that night so I could not attend. It took me a long time to figure that out. I just could not think any evil of him. I guess he was pretty upset with me because I was not catching on that he did not want me around.

He started to find fault in everything I would say and accuse me of being dishonorable. He did not want me to go church with him any more. All I knew was I had not done anything so he could not possibly hate me. I still followed him for a while even though I knew that things had changed between us. I did not understand that my brothers needed to be out of God's way so that he can work on me. I believed I needed these men in my corner in order for me to go on in this life. God was ready to take me to another level. I was sure I had everything I needed to be the preacher and teacher God wanted me to be. I was about to learn what it took to be a child separated unto God. I blamed my brothers for keeping me out of Bible College because they would tell me they would let me know when it was time to start class. I realize now that it was my responsibility to find out about class. I was really upset with those guys for a while. Finally, Christian Bible College opened a branch at Plaquemine, LA and I attended there because Sam had convinced me that I would get killed going to Baton Rouge.

I went to Bible College and drop out because I was doing nursing school also. Then I went back and forth for a while. But however, right now I have a Masters and Specialty degree in Theology. I have plans to do my last two semesters for my Doctrine Degree. So, Sam and Jim only developed my religious education until God was ready for me to do it.

I still had not been convinced that I could live without Sam. I knew this was the man that had helped me rear my children. He was always there for them. But, things became stressful for him. He needed to get out of the way but I was trying to hold on at all cost. I was still in the dark. This situation became rather hectic. I just could not understand. Well finally one Sunday, I just push real hard to go to an early morning service with this brother; and the choir was supposed to be there, but they were not there. At this time, I was doing a lot of singing. My brother Charles, another brother of the Church along with his wife and son were present. Jim, my older brother was present also. Everyone participated on program except me. Charles was a preacher. He died some three years before I wrote this book. My brother, the pastor insisted that Charles sings a solo even though I was present and sang solos often. He (the pastor) just angered me. He called everyone's name that was there.

Later that morning, after church, I was wondering why he had ignored me. He walked up to me at a corner grocery store and said, "Are you doing alright?" I said, "Yes, I am fine." Then he asked a second time, as if he was waiting for me to react to what he had done. Again, Charles said, "Ann watch yourself with Sam he is jealous of you." I still had a problem with that because I could not understand a person, my own brother, disliking me for reasons I did not know. However, over the years, we became further apart. I would call him on the phone he would not talk to me. His wife would say he was in the bathroom or he was sleeping. It did not matter what time or from where I would call, he would not come to the phone the majority of the times. Dumb I still had not caught on. I would run into him from time to time after he told me he could not pastor me. There was a time when I taught Sunday school, and then I taught a new convert class. Nothing was working because I was trying to do things my way and putting my brother on the spot. I would not do anything like that knowingly. I was very confused and hurting feeling lonely. I had everything I needed but I did not see it that way at that time in my life. It was a struggler for me to get to where God wanted me to go. I could not do anything in the church that was pleasing to the pastor because I was his sister. I knew that I could not go before God empty handed with no work to be paid for, because my pastor was my brother. I tried to talk to him about these issues, but he would not hear me.

I finally left the church because he made it hard for me to worship. It did not matter what I said or did, it was always against him. He used his influence to turn every so-called friend I had against me and labeled me as a troublemaker because I was trying to go about my Father's business. I was kicked, stomped, pushed-around, and beat up.

Yet with all those things that he has done, I still loved him and trusted him; because of my trust, he was able to hurt me more. I had so much problem understanding that this man did not like me. Just because we were reared in the same house, sometimes slept in the same bed and ate at the same table did not mean anything to him. I believed this test was more than I could bare for a little while. I thought "This is my brother we cannot be at odds with each other". This was a problem for me. But, God had my back and my brother's back. I stayed away from my church and just fellowshipped with others. It was very difficult because I was shunned mostly everywhere I went. Many who I considered to be my friends rejected me. Most of all, my family turned against me mainly due to the way my brother felt about me. Most of my family members did not think anything was wrong with the way I was treated because God told me to preach.

After some years, I returned to my church. My brother tried to work with me but God was not ready yet. It did not work out for us. I wanted all the conflict to go away. Some time went by and God started to deal with me about my ministry. I called him to talk about it. To my surprise, he had told me for some years that the ordination board would not allow women to be ordained. God was ready for me to know the truth. However, the Holy Spirit leaded me to question him about the president of the ordination board in our district; this was the moment of truth. I had no idea what would happen. I certainly did not think I would become an ordained minister. But, God said yes, it is time. When I asked the questions about the president of the Ordination Board, he went off on me. He started to accuse me of being hard headed and being disrespectful of thinking he was nothing because I had abilities which I knew not about. He went way back to our school days, which I had never given any thought to. Because I never received any recognition, I thought it was normal for a seven year old to read anything, write letters, balance the budget, and take care of bills for my mom. I did not know that all second graders did not do their high school brother's homework and do all work applications. I had never been told that I had any abilities, but someone was aware of this.

When he got through telling me what I was feeling, I was shocked to find out about all these ill feelings he had for me. I felt like my brother hated me, I know that was never true but it was a hard time in my life to have to live without my brothers however, God had a plan for me and I had to learn on my own. If God was going to trust me with His precious Word, I had to be worthy and able to stand against the wiles of the Devil. I also realized that I could not fix this thing because I could not sit down and pretend to be dumb. I had studied too many years. God was preparing me for something and Satan used the people I loved the most against me. Satan's tactics were very effective because I had to choose between them and God. I preferred to have them and God. I have lived many years now without my family just because God called me to preach His Word.

I have learned to live with just Jesus. I miss my family but I believed God was going to work it all out in His own time. I learned to wait on God. God has promised to take care of his children. The Word says in Philippians 1:6, "Being confident of this very thing, that he which hath begun a good work in you will perform it until the day of Jesus Christ." Jesus has not arrived yet. I know he (Jesus) will finish this work in me, Amen.

If I had not experienced these things I am writing about, I would have had problems believing a family could treat a member in such a horrible manner. I believe that God allowed those things to occur in order to bring me to a turning point to learn to lean on him only. No brother, sister, husband or love one other than him. I have had to live for some time with just Jesus as the songwriter puts it. It has been the best thing in this world for me. Even thought my brother still does not talk to me. I need to tell about the result of the phone call with my brother. After he went off on me and I encouraged him to hang up because I did not want to hang up on him. He called me back a few times until I threatened to go to his house. He knew that I meant we would have a physical confrontation. After hanging up, God was still at work. My husband told me to call the late Rev. Thompson. So I did and asked him why they did not ordain any women. To my surprise, Rev. Thompson told me that if Rev. Coleman recommended me to be ordained, they had no grounds to refuse to ordain me once I was ready and able to meet the board. Well, everything started to make sense. My brother was upset because he knew I was on the verge of obtaining the truth whereby realizing that he had been vague about information about women ordination. Rev. Thompson told me to call Rev. Prairie. I did call him and he told me that he had heard about how Rev. Coleman and I were having a problem over my calling to the ministry. To my further surprise, Rev. Prairie said to me that he would ordain me. I had not said anything about ordination. It was as if God was ready for me to be ordained. I did not have ordination on my mind because my brother had not accepted me as a preacher. Once again, God proved to me I did not; need my brother, only Him. Rev. Prairie asked me how long before I would be ready for ordination. Well, I had three weeks before I went back to school. We set a date for three weeks away. I called my family members and told them about my ordination. My older sister and brother in New Orleans sent me some money on my-bills for ordination. My other family members gave no help. They just ignored it. I was the first woman in the area to be ordained as a preacher. I would not allow them to pacify me with a missionary license. My brother tried to do that to me, but I knew what God had said to me. I only was going to settle for that or nothing. However on the night of my ordination service, not one of my sisters or brothers showed up. The only family member I had there was my oldest daughter and her girls, Aunt Ida, along with her twins, Jo Ann and Joyce and her son Joseph, Jr. They also gave a dinner in my honor. That made me very pleased. I felt like some one cared for me. The absence of my brothers and sisters hurt me so deeply that I let go of all of them. I grieved as if they all had died. Here I was, God had worked out a great work in my life and not any of my immediate family would take part. At the service, I learned that Rev. Prairrie had also ordained my brothers. I was also ashamed when Rev. Prairrie rose to say he had no idea why my brothers were not there. They claim to be men of God, yet they despised me for being a woman of God. They claimed to be carriers of the Word of God, yet they hated me for being a carrier of God's Word. They preferred for souls to be lost, than for a female to preach the Word. I have some problems with that kind of behavior. It should not matter who carries the word as long as the job is done. Jesus dealt with this issue when his disciples came to him to report of other individuals who was not with them was in fact preaching in his name. Jesus also stated that He that was not against him was for him and he that gathered not with him scattered abroad (Mt. 12:30). Now, just to think on those scriptures makes one wonder. What is in the mind of a brother, the preacher, the pastor that shun, that beat down me because I carry that Gospel they claim to love. If I am with them and the God they claim to love, then what is the problem? Who are they with really? Many should ask themselves this question. If it is not of God then it will come to nothing. If it's God, then it is God whom one is fighting. How great of a tragedy that is to fight the God that one thinks he is defending. I believe it is an issue of really knowing God. One who knows the God that is the one true God, he/she would understand that God is not a God of gender or self but a righteous God whom has allowed us, his children, to part take of his righteousness (II Co 5:21). Therefore God has no respectful of persons (Gal 3:28; Col. 3:11). To God, we are all his children on equal turns that is to say we are all paid for by the blood of Christ (II Co. 6:20).

It has been established that no man, preacher, pastor, teacher, sister, brother, so on, have any heaven or hell to put any of us in. Nor, can they give any of us a spiritual gift. Acquiring this knowledge should encourage one to look to Jesus who is the author and finisher of all things (Heb. 12:2)

Women have got to stop thinking of themselves as women when it comes to our Heavenly Father and just know we are the children of God.

I am waiting for God to work out the details for some work I have to accomplish. At this moment, I am attempting to set up an ordination board because women of God need to be in a position to fight the devil. We must not be under the foot of Satan. Do not misunderstand my purpose. I do not promote division in the church. I wish we would come together. We need to wake up and see how Satan is using the other sister and brother against one another. I know that we must go about our father's business while our brothers and sisters allowing Satan to sift them of everything of God they possess. No man called me to preach; therefore no man can stop me. I am also aware of the pastoral calling on my life. God will provide the place when the fullness of time has come. I really think that everything I have endured was to prepare for the work that the Lord has for me to do.

One must have a tough skin in order to endure. The only way to make one body tough is to beat on it. God has allowed Satan to beat on me not realizing I was being groomed for a job or a position.

Satan has not figured out that when he beats on us we develop a tough skin. The Bible teaches that we should "Grow in grace and in knowledge of our Lord and Savior Jesus Christ" 2 Peter 3:18. When ever any growing takes place, there is also growing pain.

Women and men of God, whenever God call us to do a specific job or ministry, Satan will send out the best and strongest demons of Hell against you. Remember Ephesians 6:10-12 states "Finally my brethren be strong in the Lord and the power of His might. Put on the whole armor of God that ye may be able to stand against the wiles of the devil. For we wrestle not against flesh and blood, but against principalities, against powers, against the rulers of the darkness of this world, Against spiritual wickedness in high places". Satan has no respect of individual. The very person you hold in the highest regard will allow the devil to sift them like wheat. Satan has a desire to sift the child of God of everything that is the likeness of Him Luke 22:31.

The elder people would say when I was growing up "When God got His hand on you, Satan is out to get you". I found myself misunderstood before I responded. These were people I had lived with all my life and now I was being treated like an enemy. It did not matter what the subject. I was wrong. It appeared as if a dark cloud had over shadowed my very existence. It was as if there was an invisible sign on my back and chest that said," give this girl a hard time, please insult her for something. Please do not treat her kind".

Some time passed before I really understood Satan's tactics. Once all family members, sisters and brothers in Christ are removed, Satan thought I was set up for the kill. He missed the fact that the growing pains endured also brought growing in grace. When everyone is out of reach, Jesus is there. I learned what God wants all His children to learn, that is to trust Him with all our heart and mind in all situations. This is not a piece of cake but it is possible in Christ. We can do all things in Christ.

Satan send his demons to infiltrate my mind to force suicide but God stepped in and would not let me come to be with him yet because I had more work to do on this side of Glory. God send His Word and healed me. He brought the type of peace that could not be found in the world or any individual on earth. My mind needed work that no medicine or counseling could fix. I had become spiritually broken mentally and physically. My body began to react to the spiritual distress that weighs on me so very heavy.

It was the Word of God that kept me and healed me to the degree of infinity on man's scale. Scriptures like Romans 8:28-39, assured me that nothing can separate me from God. I discovered that the Greater One, Jesus lived within me. Who could possible be against me when God be for me. Romans 8:31`, 1John 4:4. God was always there. He provided me with strength I did not know existed within my spirit. The best news is that God will do the same for any and all of His children at any given opportunity Acts 10:34.

Every child of God has to pick his cross and follow Christ. The love ones may have to be left behind. Jesus said any one who put his hand to the plow and draws back, is not fit for His use. We are compelled to carry our cross. In other words, things will be hard and life will weigh very heavy at times. What will we do? The answer is read the Word and accepts what it says. Meditate day and night on the Word and the Word of God promises good success Joshua 1:6-8.

I stayed at my family's church for about two years to three years. Everything was wrong. I taught the Word of God. A great deal had been taught to me by my present pastor. But, now that God has called me to preach and I am a woman, he found all kinds of faults with my teaching. I was accused of running the people away to blocking him from pasturing because I was his sister, the people was not going to like it if he pastured me according to the pastor. He told me I needed to leave because he could not pastor me. I left because I wanted him to be successful as a pastor even, if this met I left. I prayed that he would grow in grace.

I left the church and my family refused to fellowship with me. I learned what it means to be ostracized. All the friends I thought I had, no longer were my friends. Just because I was a woman preacher, no one would fellowship with me. I was all alone.

I moved to North Louisiana. I went out to find a church to worship and fellowship with God's children. I visited this one church because my cousin was a member there. It was a Baptist church. He told me how nice and kind his pastor and his members. I arrived for service on this Sunday for Sunday school. The Sunday before, I had spoken to the pastor. I told him that I had been called to preach. He explained to me how he did not accept or believed in women preachers. He also told me that he had no problems if I fellowshipped at his church but, I would not be accepted as a preacher because I was a woman. He said that he and his members had problems with women ministers. They did not believe or understood how a woman could be a preacher.

The Sunday in question, I reported to new converse class. This act was to prove to me that I was not accepted even as a child of God. If I had been a male preacher, I would not have been put in a new converse class. I had been saved for many years and had been preaching for awhile by this time. However, I attended the new converse class.

When the teacher arrived, she first pretended I was not there. She would not acknowledge my present. I had spent some years in Bible College and had been taught church ethics. I was not going to interrupt her while she was teaching. She called on me to respond a few times. I was quiet very quiet because I was listing to the Holy Spirit screaming at me to hold my peace. I realized I was under an attack. However, the Holy Spirit had told me not to come here, of course being young in grace, I thought it was the Devil telling me to not to go there. I could not believe that there were church people that would try to tear his sister in Christ apart.

The teacher continued to ask me questions so she can try to discredit me before the class. This was new to me to see someone take up there teaching time to discredit their sister. She called on me a few more times at this time. I was beginning to lost patient. The Holy Spirit directed me to get my Bible and leave. She continued to attack me. She had very little Biblical knowledge; however, I refused for Satan to sift me by playing these childish games. I love the Word of God far too much to play games with the knowledge God had trusted to me. This lady had no idea what the Scripture said about touching God's anointing.

A few minutes later just prior to leaving out of class, a man came into the class; he said he was the superintendent of the Sunday school. He attacked me in such a way, that I got up and left the classroom. I would have gone home but, I did not know where my baby's classroom was located. I sat on a chair on the corridor. A few minutes later, a man came by; I was very upset; he asked me what the problem was. I told him I had been attacked viciously by the teacher in adult Sunday school class. He just went on his way as if nothing had happened or God was not concerned about how I was treated.

I stayed there awhile longer. The woman and man came out of the classroom. I pulled the lady aside; and told her that I did not like the way she had attacked me. She told me that the pastor told them to treat me that way because he did not want me there. She stated that the pastor said I would have cause problems for him if I was allowed to fellowship at his church. The pastor had lied to me because I asked him if it would be a problem for him if I fellowshipped at his church. Well, needless to say; the pastor could not find time to speak to me after this incident. I did not go back to that church again.

I so accustomed to going to church no less than two to three times a week. I prayed and asked God to lead me to a church where I could fellowship. I been rejected so much at this time I was at a lost for any solution. However, God answered my prayer.

I visited this church that the Holy Spirit led me to. I got up this Sunday morning; I had no idea where I was going. I got in my car and started to ride. I saw a sign for this church. I went in and sat down. The pastor came out and greeted me. The whole congregation was very warm. They made me feel very comfortable. This was something I had not had for a while.

I had a meeting with this pastor the next couple weeks. I told him that I had been preaching for some time now and I also had a master degree in theology at present I was working on my doctrine in theology. I told him I was a teacher at the Bible College in Baton Rouge. I told him about myself so he would not waste my time, if he wanted to leave he can tell me now and I would move on.

Well to my surprise, at service that that Sunday morning, the pastor admitted to the church that and me that God had spoken to him and told him that a woman preacher was coming and he was to take care of me. He told the members that I was now a part of their congregation. He told them that if anyone had a problem to see him but no one was to attack me.

I preached and taught at this church for years. This pastor told me that he can protect me only at our church or at home. I did not follow my pastor to other churches when he ministered. The other ministers hated me. They treated me so horrible that I can not find the words.

There was a time around King's Birthday celebration. This one pastor invited my pastor and I to a program he had that evening at his church. . My pastor was the narrator. I was not allowed to sit in pool pit with the other preachers. This pastor started to batch women preachers. He attacked the character of female ministers. I finally realized that he had invited me there to abuse me. I did not pay any attention to him because after listing to him a few minutes, I realized he was unlearned and had no idea about Christianity. He did not" so know God".

The thing that got to me was that my pastor not only allowed this man to batch me, he pretended I was not there. He totally ignored my present. He acknowledged every minister present. There I was, his minister, and he did not defend me or acknowledge me as his minister. After that encounter, I did not accompany him to any place he went to minister. I only saw him at our church.

Well, after some time I had to go back down south for awhile. About three years later I returned to north Louisiana. I had never lost contact with this church. I had taken trips to visit my church. During my visits I began to feel and see the changes toward me. I did not deal with the issue because I was only visiting.

When I retuned to stay in North Louisiana, I went back to this church. I sit in church during service and felt the cool spirit of the pastor toward me. I confronted him about his treatment toward me. I asked him what I had done. I said to him that he was treating me different. I ask him did I need to leave and find another church. He said I did not need to leave and apologized for his ill treatment toward me. I still did not understand what was happening.

Things started to unfold. We had a revival; one of the older ministers came and ministered for us. I had to work so I could not go every night. One night I was there the minister wanted me to know he hated me. We were at my church so he could not put me out of the pool pit. He got up shook all the ministers hands, when he got to me he skipped me. He refused to shake my hands. I did not hear anything he had to say after that point in time. I could not understand that he had never met me before yet, he had that kind of hatred for me only because I was a woman preacher.

After that encounter with my brothers in Christ, I did not attend a program where these ministers were ministering. I stayed away from them to avoid so much abuse from these men of God. I wanted them to be successful ministers. If that met they were too babyish to be in my presence, I made sure to stay out of their way.

A few Sundays later, I had another talk with the pastor. He assured me everything was alright. He would make comments like, "Anyone with a doctrine degree in theology should be able to do something". I never understood what he meant by that phase. However, God stepped in; my pastor got stuck in New York or somewhere. The weather would not allow him to travel for a few weeks.

During the time pastor was away, I had to take care of the church along with the deacons. I had the opportunity to teach Sunday school. I conducted prayer meetings. By the time the pastor returned, the Bible study class had gravely increased. Prayer meeting attendant was at its highest height. When pastor walked in the night of Bible study, the first thing he did was pulled almost half the people out of the class. He said he had to meet with them in the middle of Bible study. I allowed some time for the pastor to speak to the class. The first thing he said was "I have never seen some many of you here before. I guess because I was not here all of you came out for Rev. Southall".

On the following Sunday, we were having communion service, there were preachers and deacons around the communion table as usual. I was standing where pastor usually had me to stand to participate in this service. Pastor told me to step away from the table. Everyone who knew how we conducted this service knew he was consciously be littering me. I was hurt; however, I stood there until the service was finished.

That action of the pastor caused a spit within the thinking toward him. Some of the people did not find anything wrong with his action. Others were very angry because of the way he had treated me. I called him later that evening. I asked him why he had treated me that way. He told me that since I had been away, he had different feelings about women preachers. He said he felt that God would not call a woman to pastor or do anything pertaining to pasturing. For example, serving communion was working in capacity of a pastor. He had a change of heart toward me. I asked had God given him that information or his women hating friends he acquired during my absence.

The facts are that pastor allowed certain ministers to put him position in their programs outside the church and this church was suffering neglect. It appeared to me that Satan was sifting him like wheat. He was not pasturing his church any longer. Some of the people had voiced feeling neglected. Pastor was only concerned about impressing those guys who given him these positions. Those guys hated women preachers and they abused them in the worst way.

Pastor did not feel he had done anything wrong because to those guys, God did not care about me because I am a woman. I told pastor he hurtled me very bad. I also told him since he had taken away my duties as a minister, there were no reason for me to be there. I asked him why he lied to me when I confronted him months ago about his ill treatment toward me. He finally admitted after about eight years of association with him, I was not accepted any longer as a minister there. If I continued to come there, it would be best for me on Communion Sunday to sit in the audience to avoid looking stupid. I had always participated in communion service before I was ordained, now I had been ordained for awhile, as an ordained minister I can legally service communion without the pastor's presence. However, I left because he made it clear he did not want me there.

I went out looking for a church home. One of the deacons had left and gone to another church just prior to my demise with the pastor. He and his wife asked me to come over there with them. I was hesitating because it did not feel right. I prayed about this move for awhile, finally, I went to meet this pastor.

When this pastor met me, he pretended to care so much for me. However, I was not feeling him. In other words I did not trust me. I had been beat on so much; I went back to God to check to make sure God had the right address when He showed up in my bedroom around noon two days consecutively. I will come back to my Shekinah Glory experience. I want to talk about my encounter with this pastor.

The pastor told me that he would never do any thing to hurt me. I had heard all that before, however, I decided to work with him. My daughter attended one of the meetings I had with this pastor because she wanted to meet him. He told my daughter how much he wanted to work with him. My daughter said to him," many ministers before him said the same words to my mother until she starts to teach and preach. After that they start to mistreat her and I believe you will do her the same way".

Well, the journey began. I started to teach and preach. There was another preacher there with us; he was a very good preacher and singer. The pastor treated us fine for a little while. I later found out that the pastor was sick and he thought he was dying. On his return to the doctor, he learned he was not as sick as he believed. I believe that at this point he felt he did not need us any longer.

He took over all the church functions. No one could do their job. He started to do all the preaching and teaching even the offering. He did not use me and the other minister for any functions. He then started to slander the other minister's name. He said the minister was using drugs because someone called and told him that the minister in question was seen at a crack house. I knew my attack was on the way.

The pastor would have meeting and prayer with the other minister and me before service begins or Bible study. I would ask him doing these meeting, if there were any problems with anything I was teaching or preaching. If it was, then, we needed to discuss it before service or Bible study. He would respond by saying, "I do not have any problems with anything you are doing". However, his words and action was different.

I had been teaching the book of Ephesians for some time at this point. I always tell the pastor, at any time he wants to teach let me know. It was always in his power to take over the teaching. I had no problems with that at all. He always said he wanted me to continue to teach the Bible class. Every week at the meeting before class I would say these words to the pastor.

One week I was leaded by the Holy Spirit to stay in prayer most of the day prior to the meeting that evening. I asked God, "What is it Lord?" I knew a big attack was coming but God did not reveal it to me where it was coming from. I knew God wanted me to be prepared. I was obedience and stayed before the Lord all that day. I sung, I prayed in tongues for hours, I read many scriptures. I have such a relationship with God that he would not allow me to be tempted above my means. I knew something was coming that called for me to have extra strength.

On the evening of the meeting; we met in the pastor's office as other times. I asked my question," Pastor is you still alright with the progress of the study on the book of Ephesians? Would you like to teach tonight?" He said no, he went on to say everything was alright and we went out to the class room.

I started to teach; some of the member said they had some questions, I stopped to take the questions and try to clear up the confusion before going on any further. The pastor started to interrupt me repeatedly, as to keep me from answering my class questions. He continued to ask all kinds of off-the-wall questions; so I asked him did he want to take over the class and clear up the confusion the people were asking.

I refused to answer the questions he was asking because that would further confuse the class. I told the pastor I thought it was best for him and me to discuss that subject after class to prevent more confusion to the class. The question he was asking was not pertaining to the lesson in any way. I believe he knew that, but that was his way of attacking me. He continued to ask questions. I finally, he said to me in mist of all the class that I was telling false doctrine and I wanted him to keep his mouth closed while I take over his church.

I closed my Bible; I got my brief case so that I can leave to prevent confrontation in front of the class. I said to the pastor that if he wanted to talk to me I would meet him in his office. He continued to accuse me of teaching his people false doctrine. He told me I had to leave there because I had caused him to lose money because I refuse to let him take my title as an ordained minister away. I had been ordained for some years at this time. I told him that he had nothing to do with my ordination, and I was not going to allow him to take something that God had miracally made happed. He finally told me he did not nor was going to work with me any longer. He got in my face with his finger in my face while accusing me of trying to take his church. He said that he would treat me this way again if he feels like it. I said," No" and let for home. All of this was going on in middle of Bible study.

If I had not been before the Lord all day, the way he was treating me, we would have had a physical confrontation. He tried to provoke in every way he could. His wife spoke up and said" Honey you are wrong to treat Rev. Southall that way. You should go to the office to talk to her". The Holy Spirit was screaming to my spirit to take my stuff and leave. I felt myself getting angry, so I left the class and went home. He walked after me accusing me of being hard headed and wanting to take his church over. The last thing he said to me was he did not want to work with me any longer. He did not want me as a minister at his church. I still do not know why he treated me that way. However, that is the kind of treatment I have had to endure every since I became a preacher. I have been put out most of the churches I have been affiliated.

I am sure the question has entered whoever is reading this book; "Why didn't you just quit or maybe you were wrong since God did not stop the misuse and abuse?" Well let me tell the reader about my Shekinah Glory experience. I was attending a Pentecostal church when I got my calling. We would pray every day for noon. It did not matter where we were at noon; we found some place to steal away and pray for a few minutes.

I worked at night so I would get up and pray at noon every day. This particular day; I got on my knees at my bedside; just as I started to pray, a very bright light came through the ceiling of the room. I got up and ran to the living room. I did not pray any more that day. I thought if I did not pray any more that day, God would forget about whatever He was trying to tell me.

Well, to my surprise, the next day I went into my bedroom, got on my knees and started to pray; the very bright light returned. This light was brighter than the sun. It shined through the ceiling and then a Bible appeared in the mist of the light. A voice spoke throughout the room. I knew at that moment it was God talking to me. He said" You see that Bible, I just nod my head saying yes. God said I want you to teach and preach my word". I looked over back the closet, my mother was standing there. She had been dead for many years at this time. God spoke again," Do you see your mama over there?" I nod my head yes. God said, she is going to live in you. As long as you live she will live within you." My mom walked over to me and went inside of my body. She never said a word; she just walked inside of me. God once again spoke while the Bible remained suspended in the air, "teach and preach my Word". The light with drew from the ceiling the same way it had come. There was a quiet in the room, I was trying to compose my self while trying to figure out what had happened. I started to replay it in my mind again and again. I finally came to a conclusion that God had called me to preach and teach His Word.

I was wondering if God realized that I was a woman because I had been taught that God did not call women to preach. I had been conditioned to accept that God did not perceive me in a special way like He saw men. I was having a hard time with my calling because all the people I held in high regard been against this calling. Most of them tried to convince me that I had misunderstood what God said. Some of them tried to convince me that Satan was trying to set me up. I thought that Satan would not call anyone to preach the Word of God for any reason.

I went on through the next few years teaching and preaching a very little without acknowledging myself as a preacher because no one else did. One day just out of the clear blue, I got the worst pain I had ever had in my head. The pain was so bad that my husband drove me to hospital. He told me that on the way to the hospital, I tried to get out of the car while it was moving. He said I kept saying my head was hurting too bad to sit in the car. I do not remember that; I became delirious.

When we arrived at the hospital, I remember sitting in the waiting in the emergency room for awhile; I got up and ran outside. When I reach the side of the building, I started to pray. I told God that I knew He always answered my prayers, why He had not stop the pain or made bearable. God spoke to my spirit and said to me that I had been disobedience to HIM. I ask God how I had disobeyed Him. He said I told you to teach and preach my Word. At that moment He took me back to the moment He call me and allowed me to have that Shekinah Glory experience again.

After that was over; God told me the pain was to get my attention. God said to me, if I did not preach He would take my life and take me home to be with Him. He reminded me of the time that He had threatened my baby brother's life for disobeying his calling to preach. We were having a prayer meeting; my sister, my baby brother and a few other people, my sister told my baby brother that God said if he does not preach He will kill him before a year from that time.

He decided not to preach. He started acting strange. He asks me to help take care of his baby girl. He had got married about a few months prior to this encounter with God.

About eleven months later, on Easter Sunday evening; he got killed in a car accident at twenty-one years old. God reminded me that He threatened to take him and He had taken him because he failed to do what God told him to do. I was not ready to die so, I acknowledged my calling. I knew I would be rejected once I publicly acknowledged my calling. My life has never been the same; I was treated as an enemy of God by those so-call men of God.

I believe that there are women who refuse to accept their calling because of ignorance of some of our ministered. They do not realize that they are fighting that God they claim to love. It is not their call to tell God what to do because of tradition. I please with you women of God do not let any one stop you from carrying the Word of God. Remember, only God has a Heaven and only God has Spiritual Gifts to give to you. Man has no heaven or hell and no spiritual gifts he can impart to you. I learned that over the years.

At present I am an associate minister at my church with my brother. We sit in the pool pit together, we work together, and we carry the word of God. I feel much loved by my brothers. I know that God works in mysterious ways to get what He wants done. For a period of time I did not think my family and I would ever come back together but God showed up and then showed out. I learned who God really is and what He can do with what we consider is an impossible situation.

I have shared this experience in hope that I can help someone along the way. I am going to end this book here. There are many things I have to write about, but not now. I will write another book soon. I have much to share with the world, with my sisters and brothers in Christ. I pray every woman of God would buy a copy of this book. I am sure it will help one to make the right decision. Remember," greater is He that is in me/you than he that is in the world". God Bless you Amen.

Printed in the United States
By Bookmasters